Gunnar Jensen

What if ...?

A series of questions about life that will inspire you to find your own answers.

About the author

Gunnar Jensen was born in a small town in the northern part of Denmark in 1954, and all his life he has been very interested in the big existential questions.

After working for almost 30 years in the IT industry, he is now a full-time writer.

»What if ...?« is his first book, introducing a totally new way of writing about philosophical and personal matters. The book is also published in Danish and Spanish.

He is married to Mexican born Roxana and they have two daughters.

Copyright © 2006 – Gunnar Jensen
All rights reserved
Illustrations: Hans Bager
Publisher: Books on Demand GmbH, Denmark
Manufacturing: Books on Demand GmbH, Germany

ISBN 3-8334-4355-3

To the three girls in my life:

My wife Roxana and our two daughters
Olga and Anne

… and to those who want inspiration
to find their own answers …

Thank you:

Erik Wilk for encouraging me to change my life
and finish this book
Keith Roberts for your advice and editing
Carolina Becerra for advice and editing
Roxana for all your love and
your unconditional support
Olga and Anne for your love and your
understanding

Foreword

By Erik A. Wilk, founder of the company Vision1

This book will give you inspiration and maybe change your life radically. The answers you will discover might alter your way of thinking, feeling and acting.

Based on the repeated asking of questions, it is a book of genius. The questions are the sole foundation of the book. Most important, however, are your own answers.

Read the book with an open mind, believe what you believe and leave what you can't accept right now.

I have been a teacher, speaker, therapist and advisor for many thousands of people over the last 30 years and my experience tells me that most people live their lives full of worries, blame, shame, anger and fear.

These negative feelings actually prevent us from

getting the best out of our lives. What we choose to believe will be our reality. Life is made up of self-fulfilling prophecies.

By changing our own attitudes we can change the outer aspects of our lives. A rich mind will always express itself in a rich life – as you sow, so you will harvest.

Find a new meaning in your experiences and think loving thoughts. As your life is awareness, actually all your life is about the experience of your own thoughts.

In a straightforward way this book holds everything and it is definitely worth reading. Contemplate your answers – and start living accordingly.

The era of miracles is just dawning. Carpe diem, life is beautiful.

Greve Strand, 23 July 2005

Erik A. Wilk
wilk@vision1.dk

Contents

Prologue

I have spent a lot of time learning about personal growth, spirituality, philosophy and so on, and for me it has been difficult really to find *the* answers to all my questions.

Therefore I do not plan here to give any answers at all. How could I? I don't know more than anybody else does about life and the big questions: Where do we come from? Who are we? Where are we going?

I just repeatedly ask the simple question: What if …? Though I add a few comments and reflections to the questions asked.

I want to share these questions with you because I think that you might find them interesting, and maybe you have been asking similar questions yourself.

The questions and considerations may seem un-structured and even contradictory in some ways.

However, all the questions are relevant, and only answers can be contradictory – not questions.

Since I'm not a scientist I don't think like one. This doesn't worry me.

I just try to keep an open and curious mind, while attempting to find some universal justice and meaning in this seemingly mad and unjust world.

To me it seems that there is a very important link between spiritual and existential issues and our ability to cope with practical issues in our daily lives.

If we believe in some kind of eternal life our fear of death will vanish, and being positive and tolerant, we will be able to forgive people their mistakes while having peace in our minds.

The entire world around us seems to be relative to

our perception. Our ability to fulfil our dreams and reach our goals appears to reflect our visions, attitudes and beliefs.

Day by day I get more and more convinced that this universal life really is not based on coincidence.

I think that if you look at it all from a broad perspective it might well be part of an extremely intelligent plan.

What *you* conclude is of course your own personal matter.

However, I hope that you will get some inspiration from this book.

Enjoy!

Gunnar Jensen

Chapter 1

What if …?

What if the whole universe is a single vast living being? Consisting of living galaxies, solar systems and planets?

What if these planets consist of living entities like our oceans and continents? Containing living creatures like human beings, animals and plants? Consisting of living organs – again consisting of living micro-organisms that consist of living cells, molecules, atoms, particles …?

What if these particles consist of even smaller elements – consisting of even smaller elements – consisting of even smaller elements…?

What if there is no smallest element because it is infinitely small? And there is no measurable end to the universe either because it is infinitely big?

What if God, Allah, Brahman, Jehovah etc. are all expressions of the same attempt to try to explain the all-encompassing power, intelligence and love in the world?

What if life itself is eternal? If the forms are transitory, but the underlying life is the manifestation of a huge source of energy that lends itself to continual transformation?

What if the kind of energy that we name the human soul or spirit is equally eternal?

What if there *is* life after physical death? What if the life of a soul is an eternal ever-changing journey towards more and more wisdom, love and happiness?

What if all souls are united in a single enormous and loving consciousness? So that no one can exist without the rest? So that everything and everybody is connected and that nobody can be happy (in the long run) at the expense of the happiness of others?

What if everything has to be subject to a universal law? If whatever action is performed has to be returned? Good being repaid with good and bad with bad?

What if life is not coincidental and unfair but strictly fair to the last millimetre – as long as you see the whole picture, and not just the particular lifetime of a particular human being?

What if we can influence our own lives much more than we are aware of?

What if all our perception of the world we live in is relative and can be changed by our own efforts?

What if what we have learned about nature's law is not real?

What if it *is* possible to travel to far planets and galaxies and return in a matter of days, weeks or months?

What if …

Chapter 2

Physics

Year after year – and decade after decade – scientists go on finding smaller and smaller particles, and every time they say that now they have found the smallest particle in the universe.

At the same time scientists continue to discover new and more distant galaxies and stars. There is no measurable limit to the universe either.

What if the universe really is infinitely big?

And if there *is* a physical limit, then what's over the edge? Other universes? Or nothing maybe?

In that case is nothing infinitely big?

Leading scientists (like Edwin Hubble and Stephen Hawking) explain the origin of the universe as a big bang. This supposedly gave rise to the universe as we see it today.

That is probably true, but what was there before, and what started the big bang? And how can an explosion result in a universe as complicated and awesome as we know it is?

Many years ago, physicists discovered that light behaves either like a particle or like a wave, depending on the method used to measure it.

Does this mean that you can actually influence the world around you by the decisions you make in your mind?

Scientists have also discovered that some particles

always exist as mutually opposed pairs: one spinning one way, the other spinning the other way. If you then change one of them, the other one immediately changes as well.

Experiments have shown that this is always true – even if you move the two particles far apart from each other.

The combined state of the particles changes so quickly that even information passed between the two particles at the speed of light would be too slow to reach the other particle before it changes as a result of the first particle changing.

How is this possible if the highest possible speed in our world is the speed of light – unless the interconnection needs no physical communication because it is the inherent function of a single entity?

Some scientists believe that the earth is a living being and will adjust to living conditions in the same way as plants and animals do.

They consider volcanic activity and earthquakes as a means of balancing and evolution.

They wonder if pollution is a real threat to earth – since maybe the earth will make use of balancing mechanisms before the situation gets critical for its well-being.

Nevertheless it might well be a threat to some of the creatures living on earth!!

And maybe we *can* damage the earth in the same way as the micro-organisms in our body can hurt us if they start malfunctioning?

Everything we can see or feel seems to be changing over time. Even the most solid mountain will change, solid materials like steel, rocks … everything!

Does this mean that the energy of which it was made has disappeared?

Or is the energy only changing and new manifestations taking form instead?

When you observe the most solid metal or rock minutely, right down to the smallest measurable particles, it is clear that most of the material consists of space between the particles.

What is in that space? Is it possible that this space is full of life in other frequencies of consciousness than the ones we are able to measure in our physical world?

Is it possible that other »universes« exist in these other frequencies (as physical as ours but invisible to us)? That life forms exist in these other frequencies?

Is it possible that they travel between stars, planets and galaxies without the physical limits we have in our known and measurable world? Not limited by the speed of light?

What if one day we could learn to dissolve and manifest our bodies in the same way? Or dissolve other physical things and then transfer them to distant places where they can be displayed again?

Actually a short time ago I read that both American and Australian scientists have succeeded recently in bringing about feats of teleportation.

The physicist David Bohm has proposed a theory, which continues to evolve, that all our perception of the world is similar to the principle of a holographic picture.

He claims that we make a four-dimensional projection of a multi-dimensional reality which contains dimensions hidden from us.

Does this mean that »physical« reality only exists in our individual minds?

Chapter 3

The existence of time

What if time only exists in our physical world as we know it?

Of course time is needed in this world. Without time there would be no physical movement at all since all movement of an object from one place to another requires time as a dimension.

Otherwise there would be no evolution or learning by experience, no transformation of materials and so on.

But what if time is relative to its perceiver? A second, a minute, an hour or a day is a lifetime for some beings, a year for others, 30, 80, 150 years or more for others yet again …

What is a hundred years for the planet earth? Or a billion years for the universe?

Isn't the reason that it is so hard for people to imagine eternity because we have learned that everything starts at some time and has to end at some time (because that's the way it is in the physical world)?

Are we going to die? Physically, definitely yes. But as souls?

What if there is a dimension above this world where time is of no relevance? Where there is only the eternal now? See the illustration below:

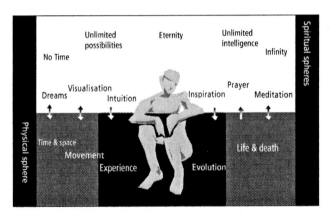

What if the links between the spheres are dreams, prayers, intuition, meditation etc.?

In our dreams we can move forwards and backwards in time, we can be in distant galaxies in less than a second, we can get inspiration and help …

What if it is possible to get much more help from the spiritual spheres if we know how to get it?

What if we can get help from these spheres to solve our biggest problems?

Help to realise our most profound dreams?

What if these spheres contain all the power, intelligence and wisdom in the world?

What if operating outside the restrictions of time makes a lot of things achievable that are impossible when operating in the physical world?

Isn't it possible to bring about a lot of »synchronisation« of events, when acting in a sphere where time and its limitations do not exist at all?

Chapter 4

Religion and spirituality

There are some common elements in all the major religions of the world. Ceremonies and the practical ways of applying religious conceptions may differ, but the belief in an almighty and all-encompassing power and in some sort of spiritual and eternal life is common to all religions.

Also prescribed moral rules for conduct (though certainly not necessarily identical!) exist in all world religions.

Islam 600 ce
Christianity 30 ce
Buddhism 500 bce
Judaism 2000 bce
Hinduism 4000 bce

The above chart gives a brief overview of some of the major religions.

In the western world today the Christian religion is the most common, but more and more people are questioning some of the statements made in the Bible.

This is partly because there are some contra-dictions to be found within the religion itself: for example, on the one hand the principle of an eye for an eye, and on the other the injunc-tion to forgive your brother and turn the other cheek.

This is actually not so strange, if you look at it in a logical way.

When the Old Testament was written, thou-sands of years ago, people were generally pretty barbaric. They killed each other for fun, kept slaves, stole, raped, tortured people and so on.

When you wanted to communicate with them, you had to employ strong methods: when referring to hell, you would speak of »an eye for an eye« – generally motivating by spreading fear.

Imagine if somebody said to one of these people: »Please don't hurt your brother, he has the same rights as you«. He would be laughed at, and probably beaten or killed.

At the time of Jesus and the New Testament, people were just *starting* to be ready to understand the message of love and forgiveness. Still strong methods had to be used. The terrible way of crucifixion shows how barbaric people still were at that date.

Nevertheless at least some people in the society of the time were able to understand some of the messages coming from Jesus.

Today, 2000 years later, many people are much more intellectually and spiritually developed, and they are starting to see the similarities in the world religions, thus getting the big picture.

They are asking whether the reincarnation principle isn't the same as the Christian idea of eternal life.

After all, the whole Christian legacy (both the Old and the New Testament) has been interpreted and distorted in many ways over the generations, by people who today would be considered very ignorant in a number of ways.

Instead of interpreting the old books and religious documents literally, isn't it more appropriate to try to understand the meaning of the messages?

After all, this message was aimed not at you but at your less well educated ancestors!

If reincarnation were accepted as the way of eternal life, there would be few discrepancies between Hinduism, Buddhism and Christianity in that respect.

The idea of karma – meaning that every good or bad thing has to be returned, every action has an equal and opposite reaction – is well in line with the Christian message that by being good you go to paradise and by being bad you go to hell – that is, as long as you agree that paradise and hell are expressions for future good and bad periods and experiences, either in this or in future lifetimes.

Then what about the whole idea of mercy? The idea that if you really regret and feel sorry for the bad things you did, you will not be punished?

Well, if you assume that good things outbalance bad things, it all makes sense. If in fact you do something bad, and you really regret what you did, you would normally also want to do whatever you can to make it good again.

You will try to compensate in many good ways in the future, thus balancing out past bad behaviour with a lot of future good deeds.

In this way the universal rule – that everything you give out comes back – still applies, but in such a way that equal amounts of good and bad things balance and neutralise each other.

Considering that souls develop from primitive egocentric souls to more spiritual and compassionate and loving souls, it is natural that some new souls have to suffer pain before they can understand the kind of pain their actions can cause to others.

So if we look at the world as a whole, maybe we are not living in a world of coincidental destinies without justice, but in a world where all the madness has a reason and where everything has a happy ending for everybody.

Some people don't accept the idea of reincarnation because they argue that the population of the earth is growing and thus some souls would have to be incarnated in more than one body!

This is a logical argument, but only if you believe that earth is the only place for human souls and that the number of souls is a constant number.

Who says that either of these two assumptions is correct? The universe is unlimited, after all, and is it really reasonable to suppose that earth is the only place where life can take root? Or are there any reasons why the amount of souls should be constant? Isn't it possible that new souls arise?

If reincarnation and karma (what you give is what you get) are facts, doesn't this give us a very logical explanation for a multitude of questions?

Such as, why some people have phobias, why you feel strangely related to certain people, countries, places and so on, why some people have outstanding talents? Why some people seem to have all the good luck and others all the misfortune?

Wouldn't reincarnation and karma help to explain all the injustice you see in the world around you?

Chapter 5

Karmic evolution

What if the evolution of every spirit (or soul) is an eternal journey towards higher and higher spiritual levels of wisdom and love? Reaching higher and higher levels within certain ranges of frequencies of consciousness, then moving to higher frequencies, then reaching higher and higher levels within those frequency ranges, then moving to higher frequencies and so on ... (see graphic below):

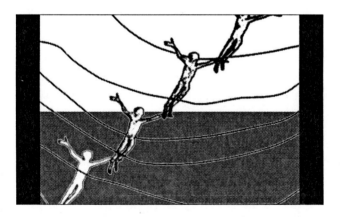

(Please consider the graphic as a way of trying to illustrate the principle only. Probably there are many different pathways to reach the upper levels. One soul might skip some of the levels, and others might spend more time on the same levels than others would).

What if everybody is at a certain level of an eternal process of spiritual growth? If everybody is doing what he/she thinks is the right thing to do at any given moment?

What if younger souls react in a way that is more physical, violent and animal-like, as compared with older and more compassionate souls? But everybody ends in the same light and joy … paradise …?

What if any kind of expectation of anyone else's behaviour is a bad thing – on the grounds that every individual is unique and has the right to behave exactly as he/she wants? If whenever you get angry with anyone, you get angry because that person doesn't behave as *you* expect and find appropriate?

When you get angry, mentally hurt or disappointed, don't you get that feeling because you expect something different from the person that makes you feel that way?

If you didn't have any expectation of a certain behaviour you probably wouldn't get these feelings.

You don't get angry with a baby that does annoying things, because you don't expect an adult behaviour from a baby. You know that a baby has not had sufficient experience as yet and has to learn from its mistakes.

In the same way you expect a lot of things from people that they might not be able to fulfil. All your education in the society in which you are brought up has created a certain idea of right and wrong, good and bad, normal and deviant behaviour, as well as a whole set of norms.

Of course society needs rules, but these are (fortunately) changing over time. What was good or bad behaviour 10, 50, 100, 200 or 3000 years ago is not the same as what is considered good or bad behaviour today.

What is considered good or bad behaviour today can vary completely from country to country, and even within a certain country from one area to another.

What is more, people have different characters, as well as varying in their intellectual and spiritual capacity.

All in all what is considered good or bad, right or wrong, is very relative and even within the same community people have different ideas and opinions about it.

This means that in many ways it is unreasonable to expect a certain form of behaviour from anybody. Consequently we should not feel personally offended when people do things that we do not like. After all, everybody does what he/she thinks is the right thing to do at that moment.

All this doesn't mean that you are necessarily

obliged to approve of whatever anybody is doing to you, but might it not be a good idea not to take it personally?

If you can keep a certain distance from the incident you will be able to have a neutral and objective feeling about the whole thing.

This is of course much more difficult when dealing with your nearest and dearest. You expect much more from your loved ones and they can hurt you much more easily, but nevertheless may it not be the case that sometimes you expect too much?

But what if *you* can't just accept everything as it is because *you* are not mentally ready yet?

Isn't it okay to be angry, frustrated and negative then? To be disillusioned, worried and anxious?

Doesn't it make sense that on your own karmic path you also have to learn step by step? That you also have to make and accept your own mistakes?

Of course we shouldn't give up all our efforts to progress, and of course we can't continue to make the same mistakes again and again.

We need to be responsible and kind towards other people, and taking life as it comes in an optimistic way doesn't give us any right or reason to hurt others in any way.

But if we make a mistake and hurt ourselves or anybody else, shouldn't we regret and learn from that mistake and then move on, without tormenting ourselves for the rest of our lives?

Chapter 6

Forgiveness

If we accept that karma exists, then everybody going through life is pursuing their own karmic path – always reacting and behaving according to their specific level of spiritual evolution.

Everybody makes a lot of mistakes, and people get hurt by others again and yet again. We get angry and disappointed with the people who treat us in a way that we don't like or find inappropriate.

People do the most horrible things to others and some of the victims can be really damaged for a long time, maybe even for the rest of their lives.

It is not strange that it is very difficult for these victims ever to forgive those individuals who did such terrible things to them and damaged their lives so much.

But what if forgiveness means realising that the people who hurt them were doing what they had to do, given their own level of evolution?

Should we forgive for the sake of the person who offended us? Maybe the other person doesn't care at all? Or didn't even know that we had been upset?

What if forgiveness is one of the lessons we have to learn in this life? *A very hard lesson but also a very important one.*

What if one of the greatest moments in life is the moment of forgiveness?

What if forgiveness is a very good way of moving to higher spiritual levels for the one who forgives?

What if forgiveness is also a key component in our ability to love ourselves?

Is it possible for anyone to be happy if he is not able to forgive his own mistakes?

Chapter 7

The big picture

What if all the »negative« things in the universe only exist because they are necessary to make the experience of »good« things possible?

Doesn't all experience require something opposite in order to be experienced at all? As the famous Danish author and philosopher Martinus said: »You can't paint with white colour on a white board«.

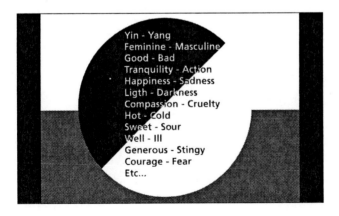

Yin - Yang
Feminine - Masculine
Good - Bad
Tranquility - Action
Happiness - Sadness
Ligth - Darkness
Compassion - Cruelty
Hot - Cold
Sweet - Sour
Well - Ill
Generous - Stingy
Courage - Fear
Etc...

What if our whole existence is based on duality as illustrated above?

What if one aspect of our whole existence is the experience of negative feelings, in order to be able to experience the positive feelings by contrast… – like peace, happiness and glory? What if happiness can only exist as an opposite to misery, boredom, fear, anger and so on?

What if gratitude is a key component in all experiences of real happiness? Or if you are not grateful for the present moment, you will not experience the feeling of joy and happiness?

Why is it that people who have everything are not happy for all that they have, while others would give their right arm to be in the same situation?

Isn't it because they are considering the abundance as a natural requirement instead of feeling grateful for their good fortune – and grateful that they don't have to live in miserable circumstances?

What if life simply has to be lived? That we are here for only one reason: To live our life, and to learn from it? To enjoy living and take it as it comes – without fear?

Accepting that sometimes the conditions seem hard, but they will always change for the better in one way or another?

What if the only valuable lesson to learn is the lesson of being kind, compassionate and loving to all other beings?

What if the ultimate wisdom is the knowledge that the only way to »heaven« is the way of un-conditional love?

Chapter 8

Trusting the universe

What if you were to accept whatever comes to you, instead of always wanting certain things to happen in certain ways?

How many times do we worry about things that are never going to happen? How much energy do we waste in trying to prevent things from happening that would never happen anyway?

If we didn't use all that energy in worrying about everything, we would have much more energy (and time) to deal with the challenges with which we are actually presented.

We would also have much more time to enjoy all the miracles around us.

If your life consists of ever-changing cycles of ups and downs, then why feel miserable or depressed?

Why not trust the universe (or God or the guiding principle), feeling confident that everything will change for the better when things are down and enjoying high moments when they come?

Because you are aware that the present situation is not going to last forever. After getting worse, it will take a turn for the better.

What if the darkest periods in life are often followed by the greatest moments? What if the old saying that nothing is so bad that it isn't good for something is really true?

What if when we see the »bad« things that happened to us from a certain distance (maybe many years later) we find out that some good things came out of it?

What if the eternal life of a soul is like the illustration below?

An ever-changing sequence of ups and downs? Some times more up, some times more down, but always moving towards higher levels?

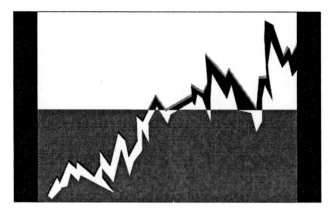

If you are aware of that, don't you have reason to continue being optimistic even when things seem to »go wrong« for you?

Because you understand that everything will be better again soon.

What if we were to live our lives trying to do our best, without worrying too much, accepting our mistakes and confident that everything is going to turn out for the best?

Wouldn't that make our lives a lot more joyful?

Chapter 9

Getting all the help you need

What if you can get all the help you need at any time? Maybe not always the help you *want*, but always the help you *need?*

What if the universe (or God) will always help you as long as what you want is what you need and in line with what is good for you? When seen in perspective, that is – not necessarily the same thing as what *you* think would be good for you at this moment.

What if you are here to learn, and you can get whatever you want *as long as it is in line with your purpose on this earth?*

Many people have lived a very miserable life for many years (as drug addicts perhaps, alcoholics, homeless persons and so on), and then suddenly they come to a point of change in their lives.

Sometimes people really need to touch the bottom before they can move forward and live a good and happy life.

Maybe they »find the light« because they are so miserable that they have lost all their ideals and therefore, having nothing at all to hold on to, are completely open to whatever comes to them?

Is this guidance from higher spiritual levels? God?

Chapter 10

Living in the eternal now

Isn't living in the now – this very instant – the only real living? The past is already over and unchangeable. The future is unknown and you can't predict it.

Of course you can plan for some things and hope (even expect to a certain degree) that the plan will be fulfilled, but are you the master of the future?

Certainly your dreams (as well as your worries and fears) will have an effect upon the future, but a lot of other aspects influence it as well.

Can you create your own future? You can certainly influence it, but will it turn out exactly as you planned it to be?

Isn't too much planning just a waste of time?

Is all this modern so-called »proactive« behaviour really that desirable? Or would dreaming and the exercise of the imagination be a better way of creating your future, leaving the details to the universe?

Of course doing nothing at all, ever, might not be desirable either?

The chart below shows two contrasting paths to happiness:

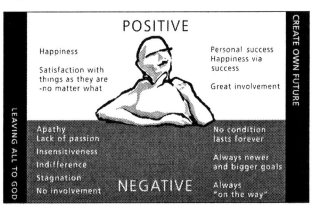

The left part of the chart shows happiness as a static state of accepting everything as it is — no matter what happens around you.

Imagine that you are sitting on a mountain in the Himalayas meditating and enjoying life, while the world around you is in total misery.

Is that really desirable in this earthly life?

Even if you can be completely happy yourself, to other people you would still seem to be apathetic and uninvolved in the world around you.

The right part of the chart shows happiness as the result of personal success and achievement.

Is that more desirable?

Being occupied in creating your own happiness by means of personal achievements and success, of course you will be very involved and passionate about what you are doing.

The problem, though, is that as soon as one goal is achieved, immediately most people are busy thinking of the next big goal to be reached.

Having one success, you want more of the same

and bigger. At the same time, it often happens that you arrange your life so that it becomes dependent on repeated successes.

You adjust your living costs a higher level of income, shall we say, and suddenly you are caught in the situation.

Thus you seem to be always on the way without ever arriving – spending most of your time worrying about tomorrow's accomplishments and success stories, instead of enjoying your life and being happy on the basis of the successes you have already achieved.

Where in the chart do you think you should live your life? Somewhere in the middle, as illustrated by the white figure perhaps?

Finding a balance, having dreams and goals and constantly aspiring to higher achievements, but not forgetting to enjoy the moment either?

Chapter 11

Illusion or reality?

What if what you see is what you create? What if all your perception is based upon some interaction between your senses and the universe, which is then compared to millions of earlier interactions, memories and experiences (including memorised opinions and influences from others)? And if all this makes up a unique perception for you, that might well be different from the perceptions of other individuals? See the chart below:

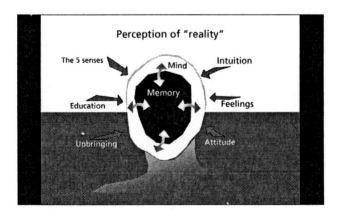

People can disagree about colours, shapes and the like. They can look at the same face, and one person thinks it is a nice handsome face, another that it's an ugly face. One thinks it's a happy face, another that it is a sad face, a third that it is a scary face and so on.

What if you can change the world you see by simply adding, changing or eliminating elements?

It is obvious that if a person loses one or more of the five senses his or her perception of the world will change dramatically.

Intuition sometimes seems to influence a person's perception of the world as well. (Some people even have the experience of a revelation that changes their way of experiencing the world forever.)

We all know that if we change our feelings or attitudes we see a completely different world. Feeling sad and depressed, we see a depressing world. Feeling joyful, we see a joyful world around us.

In the same way changing, adding or deleting elements in our memory will also change our reality.

Isn't this just what psychotherapy does?

Discovering bad experiences or traumas in the memory, and then updating this information with new and less unpleasant experiences?

Wouldn't changing our whole mentality (which actually means changing our entire education and upbringing) also have an effect on our perception of the world?

Chapter 12

Creating a positive environment

What if the human soul is creating and/or influencing the entire environment and all the circumstances that surround it?

What if a human being's dreams and longings are the means of creating the environment that will move him/her forward in his evolution towards higher levels?

What if a human being to a large extent (as long as it doesn't interfere with his karma or hurt others) can create whatever he or she wants?

If he or she is aware of (and pursues) his/her real wishes – without being distracted by a confused and chaotic mind.

What if the dreams will be realised one day, as long as the wish of the individual is strong and passionate enough?

There are always people fulfilling dreams that to others seemed ridiculous and unrealistic.

A common characteristic, in all cases, is a very strong wish to fulfil whatever dream they have, together with the patience and persistence necessary to succeed.

What if other people's opinion of your behaviour, decisions and actions were to be of absolutely no interest to you?

What if you were strong and self-confident enough to do what you in your heart knew was the right thing for you? Without fear, in the knowledge that mistakes are okay and that everything will always turn out for the best in the end?

Mistakes are often necessary to learn and grow, and most major achievements are not realised at the first attempt.

When a small child learns to walk, the task at first seems insuperable. But the will to learn is really strong, and after any number of attempts, suddenly the success is real.

Of course it is not a sign of intelligence to go on making the same mistake repeatedly, and to learn from our mistakes is the best way of learning altogether.

The problem is that in the course of time most of us tend to be much too restrictive of our possibilities. Because of the many mistakes we have made (and the unpleasant consequences), we start to be afraid of even trying.

This means that we hold ourselves back and give up before trying to fulfil our wishes and our dreams. *Even at times where we would actually have been able to succeed!*

A lot of people get more and more disillusioned as a result of their experiences of life. Often with a lot of »help« from parents, family and »friends«!

Sometimes they sink into deep depression and

can't see any way out of their seemingly endless and ramifying problems. They seem to attract more and more bad luck, misfortune, deceit and misery.

On top of all that, they can't even see the opportunities in front of them.

They are so focused on the bad things that they don't have an eye for the good things.

In the event that they even spotted an opportunity they would not have the self-confidence to go for it!

State of mind and success

Positive/High
High awareness
High confidence
Attracted positive circumstances

Positive Mind

Negative Mind

Attracted negative circumstances
Low awareness
Low confidence
Negative/Low

On the other hand there is an old saying that success creates success. This is probably true for various reasons. See the chart above:

In one way or another, people attract whatever they concentrate their thoughts on.

If they are successful, they are very happy about their success and spend a lot of time thinking about it and appreciating it.

At the same time they are very open to new opportunities, having succeeded once, and their self-confidence is high.

They actually attract good opportunities, and they are also open enough to see them and self-confident enough to go after them.

All in all a good recipe for success!

What if in the same way failures and a negative mind-set tend to attract a repeated experience of failure?

Chapter 13

Giving and receiving

There is an old saying that if you give a smile to the world you will get back a smile as well.

Most people acknowledge and agree with this fact.

But what if this principle applies to every thought in your mind and every action you perform?

What if the more you give the more you get back? What if real joy comes from giving, helping others and being kind?

What if the best way to be really rich is to give away all you have, because you will always get back more than you give out?

Is it possible to have peace and harmony on earth as long as only some people (perhaps even a small percentage of the world's whole population) live in material abundance, extravagance and luxury?

Especially if they exploit those who are less advantaged than themselves?

What if the universe works as shown in the chart below?

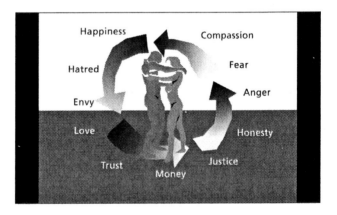

What if we are all following our own individual pathways in our evolution, but as we are part of the earth's total population we also influence the evolution of the community?

What if we are not only helping ourselves in our

karmic evolution, but also all the others – in just the same way as they are helping us too?

What if it really is possible to make the world better, provided that we all try to make our small contribution to the common need and work towards a world where justice is universal?

Chapter 14

Getting what you want

What if getting what you want is a matter of really *realising* what you want, visualising the outcome, performing actions to bring you closer to your goals and then waiting patiently for its appearance?

Confident that it *will* appear because you deserve what you wish for. Or perhaps something even better will appear instead!

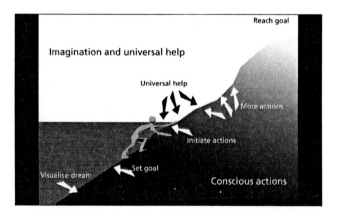

What if the chart above illustrates the »mechanism« of achieving good things in your life?

Showing that first of all you have to visualise your dreams, then define some practical targets and in the end act in a way that will lead to the realisation of your dreams and your goals?

And the universe will help you in all sorts of ways as long as you also act *yourself*?

Why shouldn't you get what you want? As long as it does not harm anyone else in any way, and does not benefit you at the expense of others?

Chapter 15

Health and habits

What if it is *not* necessarily that critical for your health to drink alcohol, and smoke in moderation, enjoying life, parties and fun? (Of course you don't have to be an alcoholic and smoke 60 cigarettes a day either).

What if the most dangerous thing in life is fear and stress? Fear of being ill, fear of death, fear of not being good enough, fear of the future, fear of the boss, fear of other people, fear of hell, fear of God …?

It is common knowledge that some people can drink, smoke and do all the things that are considered very bad for your health without any noticeable effect on their well-being or their physical condition.

On the other hand some people are trying to lead the most ascetic and healthy life possible.

They take a lot of physical exercise, drink only carrot juice and water – and of course they avoid fat, alcohol and tobacco.

Nevertheless some of them die very young because of some deadly disease.

50 to 100 years ago there were lots of people who drank too much, smoked excessively, were extremely overweight and still lived long lives.

The fact is, nobody told them it was dangerous, and at that time you were not even considered grown up until you had learned to smoke tobacco!

Nowadays almost everything that used to be considered normal (or was even expected) in all sorts of social situations is considered very bad from a health point of view, and likely even to prove finally fatal.

What if the actual impact on people's health from the so-called »bad habits« is much less than some people want us to think?

What if, when you take away all these forms of enjoyment from people, their passion for life fades and the negative impact from this affects life much more than the suppositious positive physical effects?

Looking at the chart below: *if* smoking, alcohol, chocolate etc. is enhancing people's quality of life, do you think that maybe the positive effects of these things could be bigger than the negative ones?

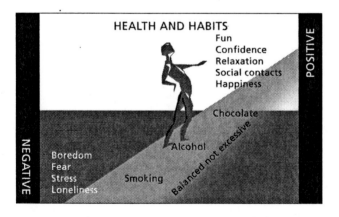

If that is the case, don't you think that maybe all these warnings that you can die (of almost anything!) is the wrong way of »helping« people?

Am I encouraging you to adopt »bad« habits? Definitely not! But isn't worrying constantly the most dangerous thing in life?

A positive and happy way of life is definitely very healthy. It can help you to avoid diseases, and if you do pick up a disease it can help you recover from it.

Even if you do get a really fatal disease, at least you have enjoyed the time that you have had in your life.

What is a good life, anyway? 90 years of boredom, disappointment and bitterness?

Most people would answer No to that.

40 years of adventure, enjoyment and love, then? Probably most people would answer that in the affirmative.

Of course these two examples are extremes, but the TV and newspapers are full of daily warnings that this or that is dangerous and you should do this or that instead.

The worst of all is that what is very healthy one day might be fatal the day after!

Everybody has to be part of the society in which he lives and there are lots of things around you that might affect your health. But worrying constantly isn't going to help you!

On the other hand, don't you think that a good laugh and a happy mind would probably help you to build up your natural defences?

Epilogue

I hope the many questions inspired you to find your own answers.

It is true that the purpose and the rules – both of life and of the universe – are being investigated by scientists, philosophers and mankind in general.

For thousands of years we have asked the big questions: Where do we come from? Who are we? And where are we going?

For many centuries the scientists thought they knew most of the answers, but since the quantum physics revolution at the beginning of the 20th century completely took the carpet out from under their feet, scientists have been struggling with the fact that the world seems to be connected in ways they never imagined.

What is more, physics, philosophy and spirituality appear to be more and more connected and inseparable.

The belief that everything can be reduced to its smallest parts and explained as some kind of a machine is no longer valid.

In the same way our individual selves seem to be inseparable from other selves (or the universal self).

Our ability to love ourselves is very much related to our ability to love others.

Can we forgive others but not ourselves? Or ourselves but not other people?

Duality and the balance between two opposite energies (yin – yang, feminine – masculine etc.) seem to be a very basic part of our whole existence.

Evolution and change also appear to be a very important ingredient in universal life.

Perception of the world around us varies a lot

from one individual to another, depending on their individual senses, feelings, attitudes, education, upbringing, intuition and so forth.

Quantum physics indicates that the physical world around us is influenced by the type of experiments we choose to perform.

In the end this means that our mind is having an effect on our physical environment.

All in all it looks as if people to a very great extent can influence their own lives by the way they use the energy inside and around themselves.

In that way we are all creators in the trinity of a creator, the creation and the created.

A fundamental question arises: is there a plan behind the awesome wonders and complicated structures of the universe – an initial or master creator? And a plan for each of us who inhabit this earth?

I will leave that question for you to contemplate.

Recommended literature

A. H. Almaas: *Essence*
Anthony De Mello: *Awareness*
Barry Neil Kaufman: *Happiness is a Choice*
Brian L. Weiss: *Only Love is Real*
Carlos Castaneda: *The Art of Dreaming*
Dan Millman: *The Life You Were Born to Live*
Deepak Chopra: *The Seven Spiritual Laws of Success*
Deepak Chopra: *The Spontaneous Fulfillment of Desire*
Eckhart Tolle: *The Power of Now – A Guide to Spiritual Enlightenment*
Foundation for Inner Peace: *A Course in Miracles*
Fritjof Capra: *The Turning Point*
Gary Zukav: *The Dancing Wu Li Masters*
Gary Zukav: *The Seat of the Soul*
His Holiness Dalai Lama and Howard C. Cutler: *The Art of Happiness*
James Redfield: *The Celestine Prophecy*

James Redfield: *The Tenth Insight*
James Van Praagh: *Reaching to Heaven*
Jeremy W. Hayward: *Letters to Vanessa*
Joseph J. Dewey: *The Immortal*
Jose Silva: *The Silva Mind Control Method*
Louise L. Hay: You *Can Heal Your Life*
Lynn Grabhorn: *Excuse Me, Your Life is Waiting*
Marlo Morgan: *Mutant Message Down Under*
Martinus: *The Third Testament – Livets Bog (The Book of Life)*
Paulo Coelho: *The Alchemist*
Sri Nisargadatta Maharaj: *I am that*
Stephen W. Hawking: *The Universe in a Nutshell*
Susan Jeffers: *End the Struggle and Dance with Life*
Wayne W. Dyer: *Your Sacred Self*
Wayne W. Dyer: *Manifest Your Destiny*

Printed in the United Kingdom
by Lightning Source UK Ltd.
111821UKS00001B/4-102